The Work of a Genius

poems by

John Struloeff

Finishing Line Press
Georgetown, Kentucky

The Work of a Genius

For Maddie

Copyright © 2021 by John Struloeff
ISBN 978-1-64662-431-7 First Edition
All rights reserved under International and Pan-American Copyright Conventions. No part of this book may be reproduced in any manner whatsoever without written permission from the publisher, except in the case of brief quotations embodied in critical articles and reviews.

ACKNOWLEDGMENTS

"Resolve" was first published in *Valparaiso Poetry Review*
"Letter to FDR (1939)" was first published in *The Green Light*

Publisher: Leah Huete de Maines
Editor: Christen Kincaid
Cover Art and Design: John Struloeff
Author Photo: John Struloeff

Order online: www.finishinglinepress.com
also available on amazon.com

Author inquiries and mail orders:
Finishing Line Press
PO Box 1626
Georgetown, Kentucky 40324
USA

Table of Contents

The Work of a Genius 1

We Cannot Recommend You 4

The Olympia Academy 5

Gravity 7

The Rose 8

Chemical Warfare 11

Japan 16

City Lights 18

The End and the Beginning 20

Immigration Service 22

Letter to FDR (1939) 24

August 6, 1945 26

Resolve 27

Mind of God 29

The Final Hour 32

Additional Acknowledgments 34

The Work of a Genius

One of Einstein's clearest memories of high school
in Germany was of a teacher turning to him:
*You sit there in the back row and smile,
and your mere presence here spoils the respect
of the class for me.* Upon graduating, he renounced
his German citizenship and moved to Switzerland
where he continued this role of brilliant rebel.
At the Technical Institute in Zurich, he skipped
most classes, used his classmate Marcel Grossmann's
study notes (he rarely opened his notebook in the few
classes he attended), and frustrated his professors.
He failed Physical Experiments for Beginners.
The professors were perplexed because his answers
were often correct, but the methods he used to derive
them were not the methods they taught.
Why hadn't he read the textbooks they had assigned?
Instead he had somehow become obsessed with Maxwell's
equations of electromagnetism. He would debate for hours,
smoking with his friend Grossmann at a café looking out
to where the Limmat River split around a rocky peninsula.
It flowed through the heart of the city and surged in two
separate streams toward Lake Zurich, the white Alps beyond.
This unsettling energy coursed in him every day. He played
violin with a blinding focus, following the stream of notes
along a journey he sensed would lead him to an answer.
The stream also flowed through letters he wrote
to young women in Aarau and Paradise. He smoked,
journaling his beloved theoretical physics. It was all
the journey. It was all leading toward an answer,
a mystery somewhere beyond.   One night
when he was supposed to be studying for a math test,
he was smoking and looking out his apartment window
at a yellow streetlight, the gray rain descending around it.
A piano began to play Mozart's Sonata in C, a rapid rise
and fall of notes. A technical wonder. He grabbed
his violin and rushed into the night, wishing to join
this wonder with his own. He found the house,
rain dripping from his hair and slipping down his cheeks.
He pushed the door open, startling an old woman.
She stopped playing, her eyes wide with fear.
He entered carefully, as if entering an animal's den.

Please, he said gently, raising his violin in offering.
Go on. The old woman paused thoughtfully, then pressed
into the keys and began again. They played with focus,
nodding at each other occasionally in mutual admiration,
fellow sojourners on this strange voyage of life.
He departed with a bow and returned to his dark room
where he continued to avoid his mathematics,
his mind glowing now with musical theories of physics.
That weekend, after a dismal math test, his parents
arrived for a visit. His father looked ill. They both carried
a terrible weight. His father's electrical light business
had failed once again. Their finances were desperate,
and his father felt there was something wrong with his health.
Albert sat, looking at his papers, then his smoking pipe
with its half-scorched contents. He hadn't realized
until that moment the depths of their sacrifice for him.
They had supported him, given him money at every critical
point. He had not taken much, but for them it was clearly
too much. Here he was, their adult child, unable to offer
anything in return when they needed it. They talked quietly
about nothing for another hour, just to feel each other's
presence, then departed. *What am I doing?* he asked,
sick with guilt.

    The next week he entered the laboratory
determined to test himself more critically than his professor.
He saw the instructions, crumpled them up, discarded them.
The other students were already at work, boiling
the alcohol mixture and preparing to monitor its rate
of condensation. He lit the flame, envisioning the various
theories of gases he'd been studying on his own, poured
the alcohol, adjusted the glass beakers. It took eight minutes
for the first glass container to explode. The bright light
startled him. Other students shouted. When he reached
for a wet cloth, he saw the vivid smear of blood on his right
hand. Then it burned. His finger, his palm, his writing hand.
Another beaker exploded. In the smoke haze, students threw
white powder, a cloud billowing around the apparatus.
His professor said nothing, not looking at Albert, as he quickly
ensured the danger was contained. Albert's blood streamed
onto the floor. Everyone looked at it in horror. His pride
told him to stay, but his logical mind knew that the wound
must be sewn shut. He wrapped a clean cloth around
his hand and hurried to the clinic. For the rest of the day,
his body shook—as they sewed his split skin together

with black thread, as they wrapped a bandage round
and round until it was thick as a boxer's glove, as he sat
alone at a café trying to figure out how he would hold a fork,
let alone a pencil.
            That night brought despair. It seemed so clear
that his life's river had brought him to the wrong destination.
He had developed not only into a useless man, but
a menace. He had strung these young women along,
pretending they were sharing mutual love, he had taken
essential money from his parents, he had nearly destroyed
the lab at his university. He'd even frightened that old
woman out of his irrational need to play music.
He looked at his violin in its stand. It would be weeks,
if ever, before he could play it again. For the first time,
he thought of cutting more of the veins in his arms
and ending his life. For hours into the silence
of night, his thoughts spun around the vision
of cutting a vein and ending his life's stream.
He awoke to the bright morning without realizing
he'd lost consciousness. He was surrounded
with his papers and books in disheveled stacks.
They all looked nonsensical. A vision of incompetence.
He found a slice of bread and thin wedge of cheese
in his school bag and ate them, as an animal would,
then spent the morning composing a letter, using both
his left hand and his painfully bound right hand
to move the pencil. The letter was to the mother of Marie.
The poor girl had been doing his laundry via the mail
service for months, believing they would get married
one day, sending love letters with his bundles of clothes.
It all seemed tragic, another sign of his wasted existence.
Painfully he scrawled: *I am writing to you so soon in order
to cut short an inner struggle whose outcome is already
firmly settled in my mind. It fills me with a peculiar
satisfaction that now I myself must taste some of the pain
that I brought upon the dear girl through my thoughtlessness
and ignorance. Strenuous intellectual work and looking
at God's Nature are the fortifying, yet relentlessly strict,
angels that must lead me through life's troubles.*
He set the letter aside and carefully sorted his books
until he found the math textbook he'd so mockingly rejected,
hoping it wasn't too late to change a deep river's course.

We Cannot Recommend You

The problem is, his professor said,
that you skipped most of my classes.
You refused to listen to me or any
of your other professors. You are witty,
you've shown us ceaselessly. Sometimes
even brilliant. But you mock what we do.
How could we possibly recommend you
for any sort of position of responsibility?
The outcome of this was becoming clear.
I will be the only graduate not to be offered
a teaching position, Albert said. His voice
shook. That famous quick mind was clouded
by his mother's voice, her warnings that
he had been setting himself up for failure,
that he was, at heart, a lazy child of a man.
His professor closed his file and leaned back.
Perhaps you are meant for something else.

The Olympia Academy

At twenty-three, Albert was so desperate for meaningful
conversation that he told his first tutoring student,
Solovine, a man four years his senior and uncertain
about what he wanted to do in life, that he would teach
him for free. They discussed physics and math at first,
then ended the meeting on politics and philosophy.
Let's read the great books, his student suggested.
Believing in the physical value of a trinity, Albert
invited another lover of physics, Habicht, and they met
at Albert's third floor apartment in the city of Bern.
Great minds, Albert began, directing them to a round
table on which sat three sausages, a slice of gruyere,
grapes, and hot tea, *break bread with one another.*
Habicht scrutinized the offerings. *But there's no bread.*
Albert nodded once in deference. *These great minds
are also poor.* The three laughed, then sat and ate
and began a conversation that would last three years.
By night they had named themselves The Olympia Academy.
They read Spinoza's *Ethics,* a series of propositions and
proofs about God and the essence of things, and had only
read the first proposition when they launched into a debate,
a chain reaction of arguments and counter arguments
that excited their minds for hours. How lucky they were
to have found each other! At nearly three in the morning,
Albert found a hardboiled egg and held it up for them to see.
Is God in this egg? he asked. Solovine: *Of course.* Habicht:
Not. Albert declared he would eat the evidence, then did so.
His companions laughed wearily. Habicht checked his
watch. *Let's stay up until sunrise.* Solovine yawned.
Albert's sense of solidarity over-rode his fatigue.
He nodded. Solovine blinked several times, waking himself,
then opened his book to a page. *What about this then?*
he asked before reading: *'If a stone falls from a roof
onto someone's head and kills him, they will demonstrate
that the stone fell in order to kill the man, for if it had not
by God's will fallen with that purpose, how many
circumstances have all happened together by chance?*
Albert brooded. He'd been thinking about a similar question.
It seems impossible for it to happen in this way, he replied.
*Bad things happen to pious people, just as good things happen.
There is no order or sense in it, not if you consider*

5

a thousand instances all at once. People are the only ones who find meaning in any circumstance. Solovine grimaced. *Does that mean that there's no meaning in us finding each other like this? Doesn't it seem as if we were all prepared for this moment?* They sat in silence. *Here,* Albert said, standing. He swayed a moment before retrieving his violin from its pedestal in the corner. He sat, pressing his chin to the cold chinrest, and played. It was Tartini's Sonata in G Minor, a soft, melancholy expression. Habicht watched, leaning back in his chair, gazing intensely as if trying to understand a strange language. Solovine nodded slowly until Albert had finished, then after a few moments, said to both of them, *Don't you see what I mean?*

Gravity

Albert kept seeing the man falling from the building.
The same vest and jacket, the same stone gray
as the facades that lined the street, the man wore
a suit identical to Albert, who stood at the window
of his third floor Patent office, weighted by sadness,
lost in thought as he often was. He noticed the silhouette
across the street and against the stone gray sky.
The man had looked down only once, then stepped off
as casually as entering an elevator. He dropped,
arms rising, jacket billowing. The awkward impact.

The step, that casual step, was what stuck in his memory.
Each time he thought of it, he felt the sensation
the man must have felt, the strangely rushing
weightlessness, the supernatural state of free
existence. It was shocking to witness the death
that followed, in part because he too had sensed
his life had gone wrong—the loss of their daughter,
the rejection by his beloved scientific community—
and at times it had been tempting to step off
into this elevator, as easy as another step in his day's walk.

Years later, when this story of the man became infamous
as one origin of Relativity, Albert insisted it was merely
a thought experiment, that there was no businessman
who had stepped off and nearly struck a young woman
in a yellow dress just leaving a café at street level.
She was startled, stumbling and falling away from his corpse,
her screams a distant echo from Albert's position
three stories above. Most often he had said
it was actually the happiest of thoughts, this man falling,
because it had changed everything—not the inevitable
dissolution of his marriage, not the sadness and frustration,
but the meaning of his scientific life, which was most important—
and this elevator was a box that had protected both
from the gravity of the world, even after the cable
was cut, even after weightlessness made them dizzy
and they were free for only one sacred moment.

The Rose

In the heat of the summer of 1913 two leading physicists,
Max Planck and Hermann Nernst, wrote to Albert from Berlin,
informing him they would be visiting Zurich to see him.
They had an offer for him to consider. He was intrigued.
At the appointed time, he left his apartment without telling
Mileva, walked down the hill to the river, the cathedral towers
with giant clocks rising above, and walked the stone street
that followed the Limmat upstream to the heart of the city.
Stone bridges stretched flat across the river every five minutes.
It was the dinner hour. The sun shone brightly on the spires
but had left the streets in half-light. Men in suits,
women in dresses, walked arm in arm. Restaurant aromas
were so thick they engulfed him like humid air, making
him sweat. Soon the train station came into view,
like a massive roman temple, its roof an arch of green
copper, enormous clocks in each corner tower.
The train was just pulling in, pulsing plumes of smoke
beneath the arched roof. Albert waited in a buoyant mood.
A crowd unloaded from the train, lowering suitcases,
descending the stairs. Then the two men were approaching,
bright smiles. It amused Albert that they looked like a pair—
both were short and bald except a trimmed wisp of hair
above the ears, both mustached, wearing small, round spectacles.
They even stepped in unison, as if they often walked together.
But Planck reached out his hand first and spoke first, saying it
was good to see him again. Nernst, his second, did the same.
Their wives came up behind, and everyone was introduced
before they collected their luggage and sent their wives
in carriages on to the hotel. *A café?* Planck suggested.
The three crossed the street and found a café overlooking
the river. It was a warm evening, the streetlights
reflecting off the dark river. Planck took in the view.
*The only reason I would choose Berlin over this beautiful city
is because it is the Capitol of the scientific world. With that,
there is no choice.* Albert nodded in agreement. Planck and Nernst
assessed him for a few moments, then Planck began,
This is the offer we would like to extend for your consideration.
Albert withdrew his pipe and prepared its bowl.
*There is an opening in the Prussian Academy of Sciences.
That in itself pays a generous stipend. But we have also
arranged for you to be named a senior research professor*

at the University of Berlin. Nernst leaned forward to add,
*There would be no teaching requirement. Your only duty
would be to continue the research you have already begun.*
Planck watched Albert's expression very carefully.
Albert had not looked up, concentrating on tamping his tobacco.
He lit it, puffing like a slow train. The calm was veneer.
His heart pounded so that he heard it in his ears. *But God
blesses us in threes*, Planck continued. *You will also
be named the director of the first theoretical physics institute.*
Albert coughed and drew in a long, shaky breath. When he exhaled,
he nearly flooded the area with smoke. *If you would like time
to consider*, Nernst began. Albert nodded, chewing the tip
of his pipe. He was ecstatic and confused. Such a strange offer—
because it seemed entirely perfect. He certainly needed the money.
He also felt stifled here in Zurich with Mileva after their return
from Prague, very far from the conversation about physics.
Would I need to become a German citizen again?
Planck nodded, then added, *But you would be allowed to also
keep your Swiss citizenship.* The waiter stopped with a platter,
on it a tea kettle and porcelain cups. He slowly filled
a cup for each, then bowed and departed. *And this
has all been approved?* Albert asked. They nodded.
And the Kaiser knows who I am? Nernst burst into laughter,
his eyes squinting behind the thick glass of his spectacles.
They sipped their tea for a few moments. *Take some time
to consider it*, Nernst said gently. *Do you need a few days?*
From the moment they defined the offer, Albert wanted to blurt
Yes! Yes! But with something that seemed so perfect,
like a loving gift from the universe, he needed to determine
if there was an error in his lens. *An hour, I think.*
*Here's what we can do. You two can walk the city some,
and I'll meet you in precisely an hour at the spot
in the train station where you first saw me.*
Always ready for fun, he added, *If my answer is no,
I will hand you a white rose. If my answer is yes,
the rose will be red.* This time, Nernst laughed
with his mouth open, showing his white teeth. *Agreed*,
he said. Planck nodded, looking at Nernst with amusement.
They stood and shook hands, then separated.
Albert went onto the peninsula by the train station
where the Limmat River split into its two streams.
There was an unlit park there. He walked to the tip
of the peninsula where the water divided. Somewhere

in the darkening evening a crowd cheered in celebration,
as if concluding a wedding. Albert's heart celebrated
with them. On the way back, he stopped at a flower vendor
and bought a red rose. Planck and Nernst awaited him,
their expressions serious as he neared. Then he produced
the rose from behind his back and handed it to Planck,
who smiled and hugged Albert. It was a feeling
not unlike a son-in-law being welcomed into a new family.

Chemical Warfare

> *"We are the Dead. Short days ago*
> *We lived, felt dawn, saw sunset glow,*
> *Loved and were loved, and now we lie*
> *in Flanders fields."*
>   —John McCrae, penned on May 3, 1914

Berlin in April 1914. Albert had just arrived
and was feeling the exhilaration of freedom.
Mileva was still in Zurich with the children.
He had no more teaching responsibilities.
He was in a city that wanted him enough
to offer him citizenship again and an enormous
salary with no formal demands except his presence.
His days were simple—simple meals, simple
furniture, a tram stop near his apartment
that would take him directly to his office
at the Kaiser Wilhelm Institute where a new
desk and bookshelves awaited him.
On the first morning, he bought an apple
and a pastry at the kiosk near the station.
He ate them as the tram passed small parks
and tall apartment buildings, then fields
lined with hedges until the large white
Kaiser Wilhelm building came into sight.
The head of the Physical Chemistry Institute,
Fritz Haber, with his round face and bald head,
smiled and greeted Albert, then led him
to his office upstairs, chatting about a lake
to the west of the city that was good for sailing,
about his own wife and son, about cafes
and a new dining and dancing restaurant near
the Berlin Cathedral. Soon, Max Planck and
Walter Nernst, who had invited Albert to Berlin,
joined them. Joyous handshakes and laughter.
They knew their extraordinary Institute
had grown even more extraordinary with Albert here.
For a few hours before lunch, they retreated
to their offices to work independently.
The Institute grew silent. But just after noon,
they emerged into the hall where they carried
this familial energy to a Bavarian style restaurant.
They talked through the afternoon about life

and science and scientific life before returning
to their offices to gather their satchels, then
continued to Haber's house. Haber introduced
his wife Clara, a thin but soft and brooding woman
who was a trained—but now former—chemist.
They all toasted Albert and each other with bottles
of gewürztraminer. It was the beginning of a very
long and challenging journey.

When Mileva arrived
three weeks later, it was clear their marriage
was broken. While his boys ran laughing
to greet him at the train station, Mileva stayed
back, allowing herself to be kissed on the cheek
before silently boarding the taxi. Apparently,
they had both enjoyed their separate freedoms.
In the apartment, which she had chosen, even
the workings of the tea kettle were distasteful.
She ate half a piece of bread with a few morsels
of cheese, then discarded the rest. When he was
busy, his thoughts lost in the final revisions
of General Relativity, she complained he had no
time for the children. When he took the children
for a walk onto a wooded hillside where they found
acorn shells emptied by squirrels, she complained
they could no longer visit their favorite park in Zurich.
They argued about simple things like when to eat.
The children witnessed it all, confused and silent.
The previous summer, while visiting her family
in Serbia, she had taken the children to be baptized
in a Catholic Church without telling him. Now,
she awoke the children early on Sundays with quiet,
harsh orders, and they left for much of the day.
The only thing they both looked forward to
were visits to his colleague Haber's home.
Mileva and his wife Clara bonded over their shared
studies in science—Mileva in physics, Clara in chemistry—
and even though their professional lives had been blunted,
they both still read working drafts of their husbands'
papers, sometimes correcting the math or challenging
the premises. They would talk quietly for hours,
nodding and pouring wine for each other. Often,
when they sipped their wine, their expressions
tightened into ones of deep concern. And so

when Albert learned that Mileva had likely been
having an affair with a mathematician, nearly everything
made sense. He asked her about it, almost relieved.
It was midsummer, after dark. The boys were sleeping.
She was folding his laundry in their bedroom.
You would never understand, she said. When he stuttered
at his response—because he did understand the desire
for a new life, a new companion—she turned toward him,
fierce. *You abandoned me years ago, Albert.*
The next morning, she took the children and moved
into Haber's home, where she had the militant support
of his wife Clara.
                    Then a war began. Soldiers marched
in the streets. A quick chain reaction of alliances
tightened. Their two countries—Germany and Serbia—
declared war on one another. Soon there were millions
of soldiers fighting along thousands of miles.
Trenches were dug, deepened, expanded.
At the same time, Haber and Albert tried negotiating
a way for their marriages to peacefully survive.
Complicating matters, nearly every scientist
at the Kaiser Wilhelm Institute was enlisted,
becoming officers, their research suddenly shifting
to ballistics and explosives. Even though they were
men in their fifties, far from any battlefield, Planck
and Haber would sometimes show up to work
in their neatly pressed army uniforms. Haber even
showed his pristine service revolver to Albert,
who held its weight across both palms, shaking
his head. This was precisely the reason he had left
Germany to begin with. Now, even his colleagues
were militarized. Haber exchanged the revolver
with a letter from Mileva agreeing to two of his
demands, then departed to prepare for a meeting
with the Prussian Ministry of War. Albert returned
to his office to try, in his distracted state, to complete
his paper on the General Theory of Relativity.
But then his negotiations with Mileva fell apart.
The four of them met at Haber's to finalize
the details of support, how much he would pay her
and when, as long as she returned without him
to Zurich. It was a bitter three hours, but she agreed.
The next morning, at the central Berlin train station,

he said goodbye to his young boys, gripping them.
It was the only time in his adult life when he wept
in public. His boys, distraught and uncomprehending,
clung to him, and they wept together on the platform.
Mileva was embarrassed by the looks they were receiving
from the hundreds of people moving along the walkways
of the station, and as soon as the boys let go,
she ushered them away.

His life became his work,
with occasional letters to and from his children.
He spent most of his days at the Institute, working
in his office in an entire corridor of offices.
He was the only one whose project was publicly known.
All the others were immersed in secrets. It was months
before he discovered, through the clues of casual
conversation, that Haber's Physical Chemistry Institute
had become the world's first chemical weapons
laboratory. The Ministry of War wanted to break
the stalemate along the endless trenches in the west.
They would use heavy gases, which would spread
across the battlefields and pour into the trenches,
burning, blinding, and suffocating the young men
who hid from the always imminent artillery
and machine guns. Albert was stunned when he first
talked with Haber openly about it, mostly listening
to the chemical descriptions and processes,
but thinking about the consequences. *This is horrifying,*
he said finally. *It is,* Haber replied. *Why on earth,*
Albert continued, *would you accept such a task?
For God's sake, the fertilizer process you invented
will end up saving millions of lives, which is the hope
of an institute like this. But now? Don't you recognize
the horror awaiting Europe because of your work?*
Haber looked at him with an oddly flat expression.
*If not me, then someone else. We all know this.
It was the same with your Relativity.* He turned
and exited Albert's office, slamming the door.

In the late spring, when it was clear Haber was preparing
something, Albert arrived to a cold scene at their home.
Clara was explosive, cutting Haber with every comment.
Albert had never seen them this way. With all their help
in working through his separation, their patience

and dedication, he wanted to help them in return,
so he asked simply, *What is the matter?* They both
turned to him, their eyes filled with an entire
operatic vision of emotion and history.
I'm afraid it would be best if you leave, Haber said.

For two weeks, his friend was gone from the Institute.
Newspapers published stories of five thousand
young French soldiers who were asphyxiated
by a yellow wall of gas during a German chemical test.
On the evening Haber returned, Planck called Albert.
Clara had shot herself in the heart in their courtyard
after a party. She had waited until he had changed
out of his uniform and took his service revolver.
What is to be done? Albert asked. He felt dizzy.
What were they all doing? How could their pursuit
of scientific truth lead to this? But that next morning,
he heard Haber's office door. Albert opened his,
and there stood the widower. He wanted to say
something, to console him or receive consolation
in return from this man who had become his friend
and most trusted confidante, but all he could say
was her name. *Clara.* It was May 3, 1914.
Haber rushed away, carrying his large satchel of papers
in his right hand.   What Albert would never understand
was that Haber was rushing to the Russian Front,
where he would kill even more in an experiment.
This friend, a fellow Jew. It would take nearly
twenty years, however, for Haber's own moral failure
to become clear to himself, when the Nazis took power
and passed the Civil Servant Law, which banned all Jews
from being teachers, judges, or government scientists,
regardless of how much of their souls they had committed
to the past horrors of the German nation. The Nazis knew
there were more and far worse horrors that awaited all.

Japan (1922)

His train passed through Hiroshima
in the night. In the hour before the sun
shocked the morning with its brilliance,
he was taken by boat out onto Hiroshima
Bay to the pine forest island to sleep.
He only slept a few hours, not because
he was afraid for his life as he had been
in Berlin, but because this country
was so beautiful. Delicate and peaceful.
He'd been in the country a month, greeted
by thousands at the port when his steamer
arrived, then guided to shrines, universities,
always surrounded by photographers,
everyone polite and smiling, bowing
in the sincerest gesture of respect
he'd ever seen. When the telegram arrived
stating he had won the Nobel Prize in Physics,
their dark eyes remained upon him everywhere,
wanting to see the man who had given the world
wisdom, offering him tea in such a careful,
precise ceremony, he could never decline. But now
the Emperor and palaces and the vast cities
were behind him. Late in the morning,
when he awoke on the island, he walked
barefoot down to the beach. The tide was
low, and the sand, still wet with the memory
of the sea, stretched far to a towering pagoda
at the water's edge. Its simple frame
was made of tawny logs embedded
in the sand, rising to the curved
roof that was now familiar to him.
Its shape appeared to be a Japanese
word built of wood, lifting from the page
of the sea, its shadow reaching toward
the dark mountains of the mainland.
He walked the cool sand, feeling strands
of seaweed beneath his feet, waded
ankle deep into the cold water to place
his hand on the hard wood, looking up
to the bright sunlight on the red tip
of the roof. From here he could see

the long beach that edged the forest,
across the granite expanse of the bay,
to the small city of Hiroshima
on a gentle hill, the sun glinting off
windows of apartments along the rivers
that filled the bay. Twenty-three years
later, he could not remember a sound—
only the peace he felt, a certainty
that no one here wanted to take his life.

City Lights

When Albert arrived in San Diego by steamer
in December 1930, he was, of course, greeted
by hundreds of girls in uniform at the pier.
They sang a song he vaguely recognized,
then the US Navy marching band played
O Holy Night because it was New Year's Eve.
When the mayor drove him to Balboa Park,
onlookers stood along the road waving white
kerchiefs as if surrendering to his intelligence.
He was ensnared in hours of speeches and
greetings before being driven through Los Angeles
to Pasadena, which was his destination.
He was to spend the winter of 1931 here,
talking with many of the greatest physicists
in the United States.
                        After a day of rest,
he was driven up a long and winding road
into the mountains. At the top, surrounded
by a snowy pine forest, was the enormous
white dome of the Mount Wilson Observatory.
The flat plain of Los Angeles stretched far
to the distant ocean, the sun an orange ball
of fire on the horizon. The gaunt Edwin Hubble
came out to greet him, then led him inside,
where the massive telescope was positioned
at an angle within a lattice frame of metal.
Hubble had used this telescope to make
his latest discovery, that the farthest galaxies
traveled faster away from us than the nearest.
This proved yet another conclusion of Relativity,
one that Albert had doubted. When it grew dark,
Hubble adjusted the telescope so he could view
one of the most distant galaxies ever seen.
He stood near Albert's shoulder, smoking a pipe,
quietly describing several other galaxies
just out of sight of the viewfinder.
They talked as they returned to the car.
Here, the city lights were illuminated, a galaxy
of stars spread across the Los Angeles plain.

The next day he was brought to Hollywood

to view the film sets. At lunch, Charlie Chaplin
was called in, and they ate together.
A natural friendship formed, as if their spirits
had known each other for years. Chaplin
was amused by Albert, his eyes alighting
whenever he tried to explain anything about
light or energy. They also both cared deeply
about the growing turmoil in Europe, and as Albert
told him about some of the fears after the war,
Chaplin lowered his eyes and listened somberly.
When it was time to depart, Chaplin gripped
his hand in both of his and insisted that Albert
come to the premiere of his latest film,
City Lights. He laughed as Chaplin convinced him.
You must experience this. Albert agreed.

On the night of the premiere, he was beside Chaplin
on the red carpet in front of the Los Angeles Theater,
both in their tuxedoes. He wondered at the lights.
He'd never seen so many, a million more than
what his father had used to first light the Oktoberfest
in Munich so many years before, even more
than when he had visited Times Square.
A crowd cheered up and down the street.
He knew it was not just for him this time.
There was a certain energy within the sound
that was new. He leaned toward Chaplin.
What I admire about your art is the universality.
You don't say a word in your films, yet the world
understands you. Chaplin smiled with his bright teeth.
And look at you, he said. *The entire world admires you,*
yet not a single person understands what you say.

The End and the Beginning

It should have been a sign when he didn't feel
the earthquake. He was even talking to an expert
about temblors when students began fleeing
the campus buildings into the grass where he
and his host were walking under the sunny sky.
Did you feel it? they called to a perplexed Albert.
The next day on the train ride east out of Pasadena,
he learned that more than a hundred people had died
from something he hadn't even noticed. What other
tremors had he missed? Ahead, his home in Berlin
awaited. As the train rolled through the barren corn
fields in Iowa on a chilly March afternoon, he recalled
telling Elsa to take a good look at their Berlin apartment
because they would never return to see it.
He had thought afterward that he'd succumbed
to a bleak cloud of emotion as they faced the stress
of three months away from home, but as New York
neared, the clarity of his premonition was evident.
Since their departure in December, Hitler had been
appointed Chancellor. Just in the past two weeks,
the Reichstag—Germany's parliament building—
had been burned, followed the next day by a decree
granting Hitler extensive power, which he used,
arresting hundreds of political enemies. A week later,
the Nazis had overthrown the state government
of Bavaria, and Joseph Goebbels was named
Germany's first Propaganda Minister.
Even the perpetually distracted Albert couldn't ignore
these signs. Upon arriving in New York, he was visited
by the German consul, an old friend from Berlin,
who expressed surprise that Albert still planned
to return to Germany. *You mustn't,* his friend said.
When Albert said he wished to visit his boat
one last time, the man grasped his shoulders
and looked him straight in the eyes.
They'll drag you through the streets by your hair.
This chilled Albert. Because it was true.
That evening when he arrived at a dinner,
as charming as ever in his tuxedo, he was distracted.
It was difficult to force a smile, even when
joy shone in the eyes of everyone who saw him.

Hitlerism is contagious, he said later from the stage,
looking solemnly out at the candlelit tables.
*Unfortunately, it has become fashionable,
for there are too many ignorant human beings
in the world.* It was then that he made his decision.
He would never return to his birth country.
The news made international headlines the next day.
Two days later, he and Elsa set sail on the *Belgenland*
toward Germany with plans to disembark in Belgium.
They would arrive in Antwerp homeless and country-less.
The seas made him ill. He spent his days mentally
composing a letter to resign from his membership
at the Prussian Academy, the scientific organization
he most admired. En route he learned that a German
newspaper had published an article with the headline
Not Yet Hanged with his name in a list below.
The Nazis had put a bounty of $5,000 for his death,
dismissing all his ideas as "Jewish Physics."
They had even confiscated the boat at his lake house
outside Berlin, angry that he had publicly renounced
his citizenship before they'd had a chance to arrest him.
The signs couldn't have been clearer—and the gloomy skies
couldn't have grown any darker as the old Continent neared.

Immigration Service

By mid-summer of 1933, he knew
something more needed to be done.
The Nazis were fanatics. They'd kill
every Jew if they could. He understood
that a benefit of his strange celebrity
was that people turned toward him
for wisdom, and they listened.
He decided to create an organization
in America to help those most vulnerable
to the Nazis. He contacted the other
odd celebrities he knew and asked
if they would help him. Their organization
would be called the International Relief
Association. Money and connections—
any resources would help. Each day,
the number of refugees was mounting.
Philosopher John Dewey agreed to help,
along with historian Charles Beard,
novelist John Dos Passos, theologian
Reinhold Niebuhr, and First Lady
Eleanor Roosevelt, among dozens
of others. He was lecturing at Oxford,
on his way back to the United States
after relinquishing his German passport
in Brussels, when he began compiling
a list of those who needed assistance.
When he arrived at Ellis Island to formally
enter the country, his list was already long.
He tried to match the Jewish scientists
he knew with universities or research
corporations, writing letters
of recommendation about their value
as human beings. He pressured his boss,
Abraham Flexner, at the Institute
in Princeton to hire Erwin Schrödinger,
the theoretician famous for imagining
a cat that was both dead and alive
based on the ideas of quantum mechanics,
but Flexner refused. *This is becoming
a distraction,* Flexner said, *these events,
newspaper headlines. You need to keep*

a low profile. Do you think the Nazis don't have influence here? This country will turn against us. Albert suffered from this paradoxical need to commit himself to his science and to help this flood of refugees. He often joked, *I have become a one-man immigration service,* but the consequences for his failure were unthinkable.

Letter to FDR (1939)

Albert was sitting on his porch in the heat of July
when a blue Dodge pulled up and two men got out.
They were both Jewish refugees from Europe,
scientists who fled as the war grew imminent.
He recognized one of them, Leo Szilard,
an old Berlin friend with whom he had invented
a type of refrigerator but who recently had been
working on some sort of atomic reaction chamber
that might produce electricity in small quantities.
Both men were somber. Albert let them in
through the screen door without the usual laugh
and hug he would expect. They sat at the table
where his journal lay open to his day's notes.
There's something we are concerned about.
We need your help in getting it to the President.
Leo then told him a story of how he had conceived,
while sitting at a stoplight in his car, an atomic
chain reaction that could grow rapidly with intense
heat, but his concept had lacked a necessary catalyst.
Only six months ago, Niels Bohr had informed him
the Germans had discovered that uranium could
serve as this catalyst. He conducted a simple
experiment with a beryllium cylinder, and it worked.
The Germans are building a bomb, Albert said.
Leo nodded grimly, then sketched the process
on a page of Albert's journal. The volume
of energy that could be released was sickening.

Since Albert first formed his famous equation,
he'd been aware of the possibility of a future
bomb so devastating that it could possibly ignite
the atmosphere and kill all life on Earth.
At the least, it could send a shock and heat wave
that would destroy a large city. But the technology
seemed too futuristic, something he had doubted
he would see in his lifetime. Now, Hitler's scientists
were committing their state's immense intellectual
and scientific capital toward discovering the secret.
Albert had worked with many of these men,
and their understanding of the atom surpassed
his own. He knew well the blinding, vicious hatred

the Nazis held toward their enemies, not only the Jews, but Russia, France, England, the United States. The horror of it was enough to make him see the need for war. The letter he began would be the most important of his life:

Some recent work by   *leads me to expect*
A single bomb of this type *destroy the entire*

August 6, 1945

The sun was startlingly bright off Saranac Lake when he awoke.
His bedroom was on the second floor of the cottage, which stood
on a hill in a stand of white pine above the Knollwood boathouse.
The sun was a blinding, shimmering circle midway to the far shore
and its dark forest. He descended the creaking stairs to the kitchen
where his secretary, Helen Dukas, had begun setting out breakfast
upon hearing his steps. The sun had left a deep blue blind spot
in his vision. He rubbed his eyes and sat, pouring hot water
into his teacup. Helen was unusually silent as she sliced the bread
and collected the jam and fruit for their meal. In fact, the entire
lake was silent, which was odd during these late weeks of summer.
I thought I heard the radio when I awoke, he said. She placed
the food on the table and handed him a heavy butter knife.
You did. He asked, *Is there something the matter?* She looked up
for the first time. *The Americans have dropped a bomb on a city
in Japan. It destroyed it instantly, they say. A hundred thousand
people.* He stood and walked out onto the veranda. No one
was in sight, not a single boat on the water. He listened.
The sun glared over the entire lake and the forest beyond.
My God, he said.

Resolve

He understood that time was relative,
but on this freezing January morning
his walk along the tree lined street
was as long and slow as it ever was.
Under typical conditions, the start
of this walk would trigger his mind
into an interior space where his thoughts
became the voice of God and he controlled
the motion of stars and light photons—
but snow had fallen two nights before,
melted for an afternoon, then re-froze
into an uneven, crunching white path.
The journey to the Institute would take
more than half an hour of treacherous,
careful stepping, and the only thing
he could think about was the Germans.
Precisely a year ago, news and photos
were released that showed the camps.
Skeletons taut with skin. Haunted
eyes. Those dirty striped uniforms.
Piles of gaunt, white bodies in front
of buildings with ovens. They were
his people. Jews. It was why he had
abandoned his homeland to come here
to this frozen town among the pastures.
His breath drifted like pipe smoke.
When he breathed in, his lips chilled.
The chill had settled inside his overcoat
and into his body. Even with his gloved
hands pressed into his pockets, a black
knit hat pulled down over his ears,
a scarf wrapped around his neck,
he was still cold—and to think
those prisoners at Auschwitz had stood
in this same kind of cold a year ago,
waiting to see if the Germans would
return after fleeing with their papers
and stolen possessions in those damned
Nazi sedans, freezing in their tattered prison
uniforms, many without shoes on their feet.
How could he even think about Field Theory

when they could only think about a piece
of bread that wasn't too big so that they
would vomit it after swallowing? And now
his friend—a German—wanted him to sign
a plea to take it easy on the Germans.
He would not only refuse to sign it, he would
do all that he could to ensure the opposite:
that their industrial economy stayed ruined
for years. They had shown no guilt or remorse
after being caught. They would only create another
factory of death. How could there be any doubt?
His breath plumed now as if he were running.
The chill only grew worse, the air more bitter.

Mind of God

When Albert was twelve, a boy asked his teacher,
What makes the Earth keep going around the sun?
to which the teacher replied, *God.* Then smiled.
And gravity. Albert was devout to whatever he believed
and now read the Talmud for the first time.
His parents were unbelievers and were surprised
when he refused pork at a Saturday dinner.
He prayed to this God of mystery, reflected
on the teachings he'd once found silly,
including the odd prohibition to eating pork.
There must be a deeper law beneath the law
that he didn't understand. He read Genesis,
wondered if men were created from dust, women
from the bones of a man. If there is one mystery,
there are many mysteries. At this same time,
as if God were guiding him into Albert's life,
a young man named Max Talmud began visiting.
A medical student, Talmud tutored Albert in science,
the precise details of the human body, and the vast
and equally precise machine of the universe.
Appropriately, Talmud visited on the Sabbaths.
Albert opened his mind the way a rabbi opens
his heart to the wordless voice of God.
He was so open that when the truth finally hit him,
it felt like death of the greatest Father of them all.
But he didn't grieve, he raged. Why would they lie
to him and all the other children about something
so important? Man was not created from dust
by the breath of God, the Earth was not guided
around the sun by an unseen hand. No action
depended on whether you believed in God.

He turned to look at his tutor, who had led him
unwittingly to the truth of this lie, and wondered
what more he was concealing from him.
Max saw something disturbing in Albert's eyes
and asked, *What is wrong?* The word *Everything*
was too small in comparison to all that was wrong,
so Albert said nothing. He finally understood why

the teacher had smiled when he had said that God
was the reason the Earth orbited the sun.

As a grown man Albert found it difficult to explain
the underlying laws of the universe, the ways gravity
affected time (which seemed impossible, yet was true),
how the speed of light was a speed limit for the universe
under every conceivable circumstance. There was no
word for these laws—the forces and relationships
that affected every particle and every thing that existed—
except the ancient words for God. And so he used the word God
with predictable results: people claimed he was a believer.
What better example of the proof that God exists
but the support of the greatest genius in all of science?
Frustrated, recalling the betrayal he had felt as a child
at discovering the lie in his religion, he offered an equal
and opposite reaction, stating publicly that religion
was a childish superstition. How much clearer could he be?

Out of this, as if fashioned by God, a challenge to his beliefs
emerged: Quantum Mechanics. It happened precisely
when it should, in his forties, an Einstein-sized midlife crisis.
Quantum Mechanics predicted strange behaviors,
electrons moving from one side of an atom to another
without ever being in between, or that simply observing
an object would affect its actions. Erwin Schrödinger even
described a paradox where a cat could be simultaneously
dead and alive at the same time. Einstein balked, telling
a friend, *God does not play dice.* There must be certainty
in all things. You only need to look long enough to find it.
And yet, simultaneously, another certainty existed:
if you crack open the sphere of a mystery, an entire
constellation of mysteries was found, each containing
further constellations. As the bones of his mortal body grew old,
he lived with this paradox of certainty and uncertainty,
and it formed the greatest, most frustrating, law of all:
his life was coming to its finite end. The unknowns he knew
were growing in number with each passing year.
Encapsulating this expansion of unknowns was the question
he had tried to escape since childhood: *Do you believe in God?*

When asked this in an interview, he reflected for a time,
looking around at the papers piled on his shelves and his desk

which contained his lifetime of work to understand
the inner workings of what some call God.
Your question is the most difficult in the world,
he replied. *It is not a question I can answer simply yes
or no. I am not an atheist. I do not know if I can define
myself as a Pantheist. The problem involved is too vast
for our limited minds. The human mind, no matter how
highly trained, cannot grasp the vast universe.*
*We are in the position of a little child, entering a huge
library whose walls are covered to the ceiling with books
in many different tongues. The child knows that someone
must have written those books. He does not know who
or how. He does not understand the languages in which
they are written. The child notes a definite plan
in the arrangements of the books, a mysterious order,
which he does not comprehend, but only dimly suspects.
That, it seems to me, is the attitude of the human mind,
even the greatest and most cultured, toward God.*
*We see a universe marvelously arranged, obeying
certain laws, but we understand the laws only dimly.
Our limited mind cannot grasp the mysterious force
that sways these constellations.*

The Final Hour

He had known about the aneurysm for years,
but the sudden pain in his chest was terrifying.
He ran to the bathroom and leaned against the sink,
looking at the dark agony in his own eyes.
His uncomprehending mind asked, *Is this what death
looks like?* He slipped into delirium. Doctors arrived,
everyone gathering around his bed. It had the feel,
as with so many occasions in his life in recent years,
like a government council convening about the fate
of the homeland. The threat was imminent and
overwhelming. Would they surrender with dignity
or fight and desecrate the entire body?
He decided there would be no surgery. It was time.
The chill of this decision settled in deep. *Will it
be a horrible death?* he asked. It would be. Painful.
But not for long. He would feel the rupture,
the torn nerves sharp with agony, then drift
into unconsciousness, much as he had
in his bathroom earlier. They watched him,
suspecting a change of mind. But now
there was no pain, and all this attention
was comforting. It became clear the worst death
would be to die alone, without anyone to reach out to
when the final agony began. *No,* he said, *I have done
my share. It is time. I will do it elegantly.*
The doctors left. At dawn he awoke alone.
Ice and fire spread slowly out from his heart.
It paralyzed him. He gagged, unable to call out.
Hearing noises, his secretary entered, her eyes wide.
The only thing he wanted was to hold her hand.
He reached for her, and once he grasped her hand,
he wouldn't let go. This touch was an ecstasy
of relief beneath a looming existential terror.
An ambulance came. The icy surge of morphine.
Once in his hospital bed, the pain began to ease.
He sat up. The morning sun gave him a little energy.
Everything was so white and bright, how could he not
feel awake? He asked for his notepad and a pencil.
There were two enormous tasks yet to complete:
He was to give a commemoration speech for
the newly formed state of Israel, and then his final

scientific goal, even greater than Relativity—
the Grand Unified Field Theory, which would unify
all of physics. He wrote on each, all that day,
taking breaks to close his eyes and feel the world
around him. The coarse fabric of his hospital blanket.
The chemical aroma of ethyl alcohol. Then his son
Hans appeared, somehow, from his home in California.
He gripped his hand, which seemed to trigger a special
light in his son's eyes. They talked. When eventually
there came a period of silence, he looked at his newly
written papers. *My math isn't enough,* he said.
The thought settled into his body. He had long known
that with each year that passed, an old man spent
more time facing the deaths of old friends, until only
his own death remained. He just hadn't suspected
that last friend would be mathematics. He closed
his eyes again. Then everyone was gone. It was night.
He grew tired. Just after one in the morning,
he awoke with a start. The pain was blinding.
He called out into the dark. What was it he said?
His nurse, who hurried to his room, would have
asked, if only she knew how to speak the language
   of the dead.

Additional Acknowledgements

My deepest thanks go to the Seaver Dean's office at Pepperdine University for their generous support of my research and travel to Berlin, Prague, Princeton University, and the Institute for Advanced Study, as well as key locations throughout Switzerland, in preparation for writing this book. Additional thanks go to the staff at both the Princeton University Library and the Shelby White and Leon Levy Archives Center at the Institute for Advanced Study.

Historians of Albert Einstein will recognize that this book is an interpretation of Einstein's life based on a close reading of the available memoirs, letters, news accounts, and biographies.

A brief section of the last stanza of "The Work of a Genius" is derived from Einstein's letter to the mother of Marie Winteler in 1897.

Einstein's remarks on Hitlerism in "The End and the Beginning" were made at a reception in New York on March 16, 1933. Source: *The New York Times*.

Much of the last stanza of "Mind of God" is derived from Einstein's response to the question, "Do you believe in God?" Source: G. S. Viereck, *Glimpses of the Great* (1930).

This transformative work constitutes a "fair use" of any copyrighted material as provided for in section 107 of the U.S. Copyright Law.

John Struloeff grew up in the mountainous rainforests of northwestern Oregon. His debut poetry collection, *The Man I Was Supposed to Be*, was published by Loom Press in 2008, with individual poems in *The Atlantic, The Southern Review, Prairie Schooner, ZYZZYVA, PN Review,* and elsewhere. His awards include a Stegner Fellowship from Stanford University, an NEA Literature Fellowship, a Sozopol Seminars Fiction Fellowship from the Elizabeth Kostova Foundation (Bulgaria), and both the Weldon Kees and Tennessee Williams Scholarships. He has taught at Stanford University and the University of Nebraska-Lincoln where he received both his MA and PhD in English. Currently he directs the creative writing program and is an associate professor of English and Creative Writing at Pepperdine University in Malibu, California.

www.ingramcontent.com/pod-product-compliance
Lightning Source LLC
LaVergne TN
LVHW041504070426
835507LV00012B/1318